The spoilt holiday

Lucy had been looking forward to her holiday for
weeks. She was going to the seaside, and Lucy
loved the sea. She loved the crunching sound the
waves made as they chased her up the sand. She
loved playing in the rock-pools, and building
sandcastles, but that wasn't the best part.

Lucy and her Mum were going to stay on a farm
near the seaside. There would be chickens to feed,
ducks on the pond, and cows and sheep in the fields.
That wasn't the best part either.

There was a pony on the farm, and Lucy was going
to ride it. That was the best part. Lucy loved
ponies. She had dozens of toy ones but she had
never been on a real one.

Mum opened Lucy's case. 'What on earth have you
put in here?' she asked. 'It weighs a tonne!'

'Only a few of my ponies,' said Lucy.

'But you can't take all these!' said Mum. 'There's
no room for your clothes.'

'I won't need many clothes at the seaside,' replied Lucy.

When Mum had loaded the car, she sat at the kitchen
table and looked at the road atlas. 'Right,' she
said, 'I think we've got everything. It's going to
be a long drive, so I hope you're taking plenty
of things to do in the car.'

Lucy got into the car but, just as Mum was
locking the front door, the phone rang.

'Oh no!' groaned Lucy.

'I'll have to answer it,' said Mum. 'It may be
important.' She went back into the house.

Mum was a long time. Lucy began to feel grumpy.
'I wonder why she's taking so long,' thought Lucy.
'I don't want to miss my first pony ride.'

At last Mum came out of the house and locked the
door. She looked worried as she got into the
driving seat.

'There's something wrong, isn't there?' asked Lucy.

'I'm afraid so,' Mum replied. 'It's Uncle Walter.
He's had a fall. We're going to have to look after
him for a few days.'

4

'But we can't!' cried Lucy. 'We're going on holiday. What about my pony riding?'

Mum shook her head. 'I'm afraid that some things are more important than holidays and ponies.'

Lucy tried not to cry. 'Nothing is more important than a pony,' she said.

'Look, Lucy, I'm sorry,' said Mum. 'Uncle Walter has nobody else to look after him. We can't leave him on his own, can we?'

'I suppose not,' sighed Lucy.

It was a long drive to Uncle Walter's house. It was raining when Lucy and Mum arrived. Lucy had cheered up a little. She liked Uncle Walter and she liked his big old house. There were plenty of rooms to explore.

Uncle Walter was very pleased to see them. 'I'm sorry your holiday has been spoilt,' he said. 'You must be very disappointed, Lucy. With luck, I'll be up and about in a few days. Then you'll be able to go to the farm.'

Lucy had her own room at the top of the house.
She unpacked her suitcase and put her clothes away.
A creaking noise was coming from the next room.

'That's funny,' she thought. 'I'd better go and
see what's making that noise.'

She opened the door of the room next to hers and
went inside. It was full of old furniture and
pictures. At the far end of the room was something
covered by a white dust-sheet.

'I wonder what that can be,' thought Lucy. She
crossed the room and lifted the corner of the
sheet. Under the sheet was the most wonderful
thing Lucy had ever seen.

'A rocking horse!' she gasped.

She wasn't quite right. It was a horse, a
beautifully carved wooden horse, with faded black
paintwork and a red saddle and reins. It was too
big to be a rocking horse and it had no rockers.

At tea-time, Lucy asked Uncle Walter about the
black horse. He winked at Mum and laughed. 'Oh,
you discovered him, did you? I was going to tell
you about him as I know how fond of horses you are.'
'Where did he come from?' asked Mum.
'A roundabout,' said Uncle Walter. 'I bought him
years ago. He was going to be chopped up for fire-
wood, but I saved him. He must be lonely up there.
I hope you'll ride him sometimes, Lucy.'

Before she went to bed, Lucy went to see the
horse again. 'I've brought you a sugar-lump,'
she said. 'Tomorrow, we'll go for a long ride. We
might even go to the seaside.'

Lucy was in bed, asleep. The moonlight was
streaming into her bedroom. Suddenly, she woke up.
She heard the creaking noise. She got out of bed
and went out on to the landing. Then she tip-toed
towards the horse's room.

Lucy pushed open the door and turned on the
light. 'That's funny,' she said, 'the sugar-lump
has gone. He must have eaten it.' She didn't feel
a bit tired. 'Perhaps I'll have a little ride now.
Then I'll go back to bed.'

But the horse was much too high for Lucy to
reach. She looked around for something to stand
on. 'That pile of books will do,' she thought.

Climbing on to the horse's back wasn't easy, but
at last she managed it.

Lucy felt very high up on the horse's back.
She put her feet in the stirrups and picked up
the reins. 'I wish you'd take me to the seaside,'
she whispered.

The light in the room seemed to grow brighter.
The wall in front of her disappeared. Outside it
was a bright, sunny day. Lucy felt the warmth on
her face and the breeze blowing into the room.

The horse moved. He lifted his head and snorted.
Lucy tightened her grip on the reins.

The horse took a few unsteady steps to
the gap where the wall had been. Lucy
wondered if she could get off. She had never
ridden before and she didn't feel safe. The garden
was a long way below.

'I hope he's not going to jump,' gasped Lucy.
The horse shook his head and pawed the ground with
his hoof. Suddenly he was off. Lucy fell forward
in the saddle and hung on to his thick black mane.
Instead of falling down into the garden the horse
rose into the air.

Faster and faster the black horse galloped across
the sunny sky. After a few minutes Lucy stopped
being afraid and looked down on the town below.
She could see a river, shining like silver apple
peel in the sunlight. Down and down went the horse
until his hooves splashed the surface of the water.
Then he galloped along the river. Soon they came
to the place where the river grew wide and ran
into the sea. The horse galloped on, leaping
over the waves.

A fishing boat was bobbing around in the
bay. The fishermen looked very surprised to
see a little girl riding a horse towards them.

'Where are you going?' shouted one of the men.

'I don't know,' shouted Lucy, 'but it's fun!'

Far away, across the bay, Lucy could see tall
cliffs and a long sandy beach. When the horse
reached the beach he stopped near a smooth, round
rock and let her climb down.

Lucy had a wonderful time. She looked for crabs
and tiny fish in the rock pools. She paddled in
the sea and climbed on the slippery green rocks.

All the time she was playing, the horse waited
patiently by the rock. When, at last, he lifted his
head and snorted, Lucy knew that it was time to
go home. She climbed on to his back, put her feet
into the stirrups, and picked up the reins again.

Back across the bay they went, along the river,
high into the sky and down to the house.

Next morning, after breakfast, Lucy went to
see Uncle Walter. 'You didn't tell me that horse
was magic,' she said.

'I didn't need to,' smiled Uncle Walter. 'I
knew you'd find out for yourself.'

'Will he take me anywhere I want to go?' asked
Lucy. 'Last night we went to the seaside.'

'Of course he will,' replied the old man. 'You
just have to ask him nicely. Oh, and you mustn't
tell anybody about him. It must be your secret.'

That night Lucy went to bed early. She was going
to India to watch tigers.

The next night she went to the North Pole and saw
some polar bears.

20

The holiday was almost over before Uncle Walter
was better. There was no time left for Lucy and
Mum to go to the farm.

'I must say you've been a very good girl,'
said Mum. 'I thought you were going
to be upset about missing your
holiday. You'd been looking forward
to it so much.'

'But I'm having a lovely time here,'
said Lucy. 'It's much nicer than the
seaside. I wish we didn't have to
go home.'

When she went back to school Lucy wanted to tell
her friends about the horse. However, she remembered
what Uncle Walter had said, and kept her adventures
secret.

One morning Lucy was getting ready for school
when the doorbell rang. 'It's for you, Lucy,'
called Mum.

A big red van had pulled up outside and two
men were lifting a huge parcel out of the back.

'It's from Uncle Walter,' smiled Mum. 'I expect
you can guess what it is.'

All about horses

Today's horses come from much smaller animals that lived on earth millions of years ago.

Zebras and donkeys also come from these small animals. We say that they are members of the horse family.

A long, long time ago, people learned how to tame horses. Before there were cars, people would travel from place to place on horses. Horses are much stronger than humans. Before there were lorries, heavy loads were pulled by horses.

Before there were tractors, horses worked on farms.

Ponies used to work down coal mines. Can you think why ponies were better than horses for this work?

Today, horses and ponies are used for pleasure;
and in sport.

Horses are beautiful animals.
Since earliest times artists have drawn or
painted horses or made statues of them.

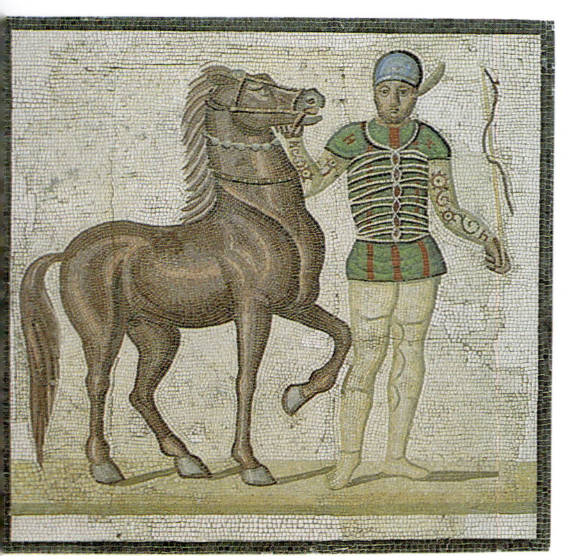

The most famous horse in the world

King Philip had been buying horses for the royal
stables. When the sale was over, he went to look
at the beautiful animals he had bought.

'You've bought some fine horses today, Sir,'
said one of the grooms.

'I suppose I have,' replied Philip, 'but I'm
still not satisfied. I was hoping to find something
extra special. A horse fit for a king.'

At that moment he saw the very creature he had
been describing. It was being led away by one of
the stable-boys.

28

'Stop!' shouted the King. 'Isn't that horse for
sale? Why didn't you show him to me?'

'I was afraid to,' replied the boy. 'My Master
dare not sell him. This horse has such a fiery
temper that nobody can tame him. Anybody who tries
to ride him is sure to get hurt.'

'We'll see about that,' laughed the King. 'Take
him into the ring.'

Many of the King's men tried to control the horse
but nobody could. As they went near the animal
it kicked, and reared, and snorted in terror.

The King's young son, Alexander, had been watching.
'I'll bet I can ride him,' he said.

'Nonsense!' snapped his father. 'You wouldn't
get near him. My best horsemen have failed.'

'If I can tame him, will you buy him for me?'
asked Alexander.

The King thought for a long time. Then he smiled.

'Yes, I will,' he said.

The King's son walked into the ring. He spoke to
the men who were holding the horse. 'Turn him around,'
he said, 'so that he can't see his shadow.'

The boy had seen that the horse was frightened of its shadow. He spoke softly to the animal and stroked its nose. He sent the grooms out of the ring and walked the horse a few paces. He could sense that it was beginning to trust him.

After a while he climbed on to the animal's back. The horse didn't rear or kick or try to throw him. He patted the horse's neck and spoke softly in its ear. For a while the horse stood very still. Then it began to walk slowly round the ring.

Soon the boy was riding calmly and expertly.

'Well done, Alex!' shouted the King. 'The horse is yours. What are you going to call him?'

'Oxhead,' replied Alexander.

When Alexander grew up he became the greatest king the world had ever known. Oxhead went everywhere with him. When Oxhead died Alexander was heart-broken. He wanted his horse to be remembered forever so he built a great city and called it Oxheadtown in memory of his beloved horse.